ENERGY
IS THE
REAL GOD

RAJINDER SHARMA

BALBOA.PRESS
A DIVISION OF HAY HOUSE

Copyright © 2020 Rajinder Sharma.

All rights reserved. No part of this book may be used or reproduced by any means, graphic, electronic, or mechanical, including photocopying, recording, taping or by any information storage retrieval system without the written permission of the author except in the case of brief quotations embodied in critical articles and reviews.

Balboa Press books may be ordered through booksellers or by contacting:

Balboa Press
A Division of Hay House
1663 Liberty Drive
Bloomington, IN 47403
www.balboapress.co.uk
UK TFN: 0800 0148647 (Toll Free inside the UK)
UK Local: 02036 956325 (+44 20 3695 6325 from outside the UK)

Because of the dynamic nature of the Internet, any web addresses or links contained in this book may have changed since publication and may no longer be valid. The views expressed in this work are solely those of the author and do not necessarily reflect the views of the publisher, and the publisher hereby disclaims any responsibility for them.

The author of this book does not dispense medical advice or prescribe the use of any technique as a form of treatment for physical, emotional, or medical problems without the advice of a physician, either directly or indirectly. The intent of the author is only to offer information of a general nature to help you in your quest for emotional and spiritual well-being. In the event you use any of the information in this book for yourself, which is your constitutional right, the author and the publisher assume no responsibility for your actions.

Any people depicted in stock imagery provided by Getty Images are models, and such images are being used for illustrative purposes only. Certain stock imagery © Getty Images.

Print information available on the last page.

ISBN: 978-1-9822-8255-4 (sc)
ISBN: 978-1-9822-8256-1 (e)

Balboa Press rev. date: 11/13/2020

Contents

Dedication vii
Preface ix

Chapter 1 Human concepts 1
Chapter 2 Unbelievable origin of life 19
Chapter 3 Different forms of life on Earth 27
Chapter 4 Plagues created by humans 34
Chapter 5 Mysteries of human sports 41
Chapter 6 Creation, evolution and termination of life ... 45
Chapter 7 The scientific God 51
Chapter 8 My ten commandments 56

Addendum 1 Foreign words 61
Addendum 2 The book cover 63

Dedication

Amongst the humans, I have the greatest respect for Albert Einstein who had incredibly created a simple formula about the most complex concept in human minds. Strangely, he himself had not realized that, what he had created, reveals the very origin of life, which is something that no human had ever managed to fathom. To me, Einstein's formula reveals that there is life in the entire universe. My dedication to Einstein is to educate all the humans on our planet what Einstein's thinking that has revealed to me.

My life is also dedicated to numerous lifeforms on my beautiful planet. It has been a privilege for me to have been on a planet that is delightfully populated by an enormous variety of lifeforms. I cannot imagine that such a variety of life is likely anywhere else in our universe.

mmxx

Dedication

Preface

My recollection of my own life resulted in me thinking about the major change of human life that has occurred during my lifetime. We humans may have been the most advanced species of life on our wonderful planet, but currently we have started creating more problems, not just for ourselves but also for the numerous other lifeforms on our wonderful planet. We are not even aware that the concepts created in our heads are plaguing the whole of our unique planet.

During my life, there were disasters that made me experience being in hell. Also, during my life, there were disasters that placed me in a better state of existence than what I had been experiencing before. That then made me recognise that, most of my normal existence on my planet had been unique because no other existence on my planet could or would have experienced what I have. My book is to alert humans that you yourself should become aware of your own existence on the most wonderful planet in the universe and to recognise that heaven and hell can only be experienced during our lives on our planet and not somewhere else. I advise readers not to pack their bags for some weird existence after their lives here.

Some of my explanations may shock some readers, but my desire is to help people to become aware of the situations that are created solely by us humans and are affecting not only our lives but also terminating the existence of numerous other forms of life on our unique planet. Humans may not be aware that our lives will be overtaken by another form of life that is currently being triggered by our life activities. That it is most likely to be happening in the next century.

During my life there had been many mysteries. I never imagined that they could ever be solved. Those included:

- Where did the universe come from?
- Why is our planet only a speck in the universe?
- What started life on our planet?
- Why is the origin of life?
- What on earth is a God?
- What could be there after death?
- What on earth brought my parents and me into existence?

Strangely, during the final stage of my existence, I managed to solve all the mysteries that had been in my head during my life. That resulted in me deciding to enable people to open their minds to our existence on a unique planet in our universe.

My thanks are to all the long-lasting atoms on my planet that have been part of my body during the whole period of my short existence.

1

HUMAN CONCEPTS

Religions

It was in 1939 that I was born in a part of Africa that was a British colony. My parents were an Indian Hindu family and my neighbourhood had people with different religious beliefs. In Hinduism, there are many paths for God worship. Some Indian families in our neighbourhood went to the Hindu temples that had various statues in them. The Arya Samaj group that did not associate with temples and statues. My father and most of our Hindu neighbours from the Punjab were in that sect. Our Arya Samaj sect of Hinduism had been originated by the Aryans arriving in India about twelve thousand years ago from northern Asia due to polar ice spreading southwards. Some Aryans went to Europe and integrated with various other humans. Our Arya Samaj ceremonies in Mombasa were carried out beside a small fire at the gathering centres and in our homes.

Hinduism absorbed various beliefs and paths of worship for God providing they were totally peaceful. My mother was from a family that also went to temples. Together with her and my Hindu friends, I also used to go to Hindu temples that had statues. Hinduism uses the swastika as a peaceful symbol and believes that we ourselves had been through all other animal lifeforms as well. That is why most Hindus are vegetarians and always tend to show respect to all other lifeforms on our planet. Hinduism taught me that my misdeeds in life could result in a lower state of existence for my next life.

Directly opposite us lived the Christian family that had originally come from the Seychelles Island in the Indian Ocean. Two other Christian families living close to our neighbourhood were Goans from India. The Christians did the regular church goings on Sundays and would dress up smartly for the occasion. I remember a Seychellois boy telling me that at the end of the prayers in church he would be given a little sweet that was being created by Jesus Christ in the church. At Christmas time, they would have celebrations that were totally different to our Hindu celebrations of *Diwali* which was linked to lunar calendars. We usually exchanged various kinds of sweets during those religious days.

In the large house to our right there were two Muslim families. In one family, the man had three wives. Muslim celebrations were on the holy days of *Eid* festivals. On one of those days there would be a slaughtering of a goat in their back yard right next to our house. Although we had a separating fence between us, I had seen the slaughtered goat hanging upside down and draining away its blood.

In the house to the right of the one opposite us, there lived a Sikh family. Sikhism had emerged from a mixture of Hindu and Muslim beliefs. There are visual indications on the bodies of the men to indicate their link to Sikhism. These are specified by five k's in Punjabi which translate to hair, comb, sword, underpants and metal wrist bangle. That is why men do not cut their hair on the head but roll it up, plug a little comb in it and cover their heads with a turban. Their sword was their method of protecting themselves against any physical threat from other religions. In Mombasa, many Africans had become Muslims and some became Christians, but a lot of them had some African beliefs of which I know little. The magic dance called '*ganga*' in their gatherings could be some religious belief.

The strangest thing was that Hinduism was a religion in which a person was born and not one that was passed to other people. There were within Hinduism many different paths of worship and different symbols for God. Amazingly, no group objected to any of

Energy is the Real God

the other approaches that were very different to the others in the same religion. The various God symbols provided a suitable path for various mentalities in the masses. During my childhood, I had learnt some Hindu prayers and would sit on a small wooden plank called *pattada* in Punjabi. Then I would go through the Hindi prayers in my mind. There could be people walking past me. There also were times when I would say some prayers in my head while playing marbles to help me to win. There was no doubt that the prayers in my head helped me win marbles. I was devoted to my praying as it helped me to be successful in my school and play activities. Although there were times when I could not achieve what I was trying to achieve I felt that my God must be thinking about my future. Most of the time there was no image of the God that I was praying to. Sometimes there were the images of Rama and Krishna, the two incarnations of the Hindu God of preservation. Amongst the people living around me there were other religions which preached different pathways to a God that was different to my God. However, our different religious beliefs never created any problems in our friendships.

One day at my high school I was thrilled by a geography lesson about the Earth being a planet in a solar system. I then became thrilled by the sight of stars at night although astronomy was not taught to us at school. All through my life my knowledge of the sky visions continued to increase. I could not believe that I was looking at my universe in which we existed. That made me feel that my God had more than just our Earth to look after. Then I started finding it difficult to conceive God being the creator of a planet where numerous disasters were occurring and lifeforms were killing and eating other lifeforms for their survival. God started becoming a puzzle in my life.

The Hindu God teachings seemed to be like ancient Greek mythology. In Hinduism, there is the concept of a trinity of God although the Creator of that trinity is unimaginable. The trinities are made up of male/female Gods for creation, preservation and termination of life. The preservation God Vishnu and Lakshmi had incarnations of Rama and Krishna whose lives are depicted in the religious books, the *Ramayan* and the *Geeta*, which to me then became myth stories. It was later in my life that I learnt that there were nine incarnations of that preservation God. It was intriguing that all the incarnations were not just humans, but even some creatures in the sea. The first four incarnations were:

1. Fish   *Matsya*   in water
2. Tortoise   *Kurma*   in water & on land
3. Boar   *Varaha*   on land
4. Human-head lion *Narasimha*   on land

The four animal incarnations of God are similar in form to the later human concept of the evolutionary life on our planet that only dawned on humans more than two thousand years after the Hindu conceptions of life. Hindus have a great respect for all animal life forms on our planet and led most of them to be vegetarians. Rama and Krishna were the human incarnations of the preservation God that followed the animals. After a suitable behaviour during our final life, we humans could then return to being with our unimaginable God called *Bugawaan* for which there is no image. Those ancient Hindu concepts of God amazingly fitted in with our later scientific understanding of our evolutionary linkage with all other lifeforms on our planet.

On our planet there were different religious beliefs because they were created by humans who lived in different parts of a flat earth. No religious beliefs had any answers for the disasters that are destroying lives of people and animals at random. Any of the religions that are totally peaceful with their beliefs are totally acceptable. However, I cannot accept the pathetic behaviour of some religious beliefs that originated in the Middle East that are trying to force their beliefs into others human minds or go around killing humans who have different beliefs around the whole globe and kill humans who have some differences in the same religion. Even though our scientific advances can explain our universe and the causes of the natural disasters, we are totally failing to deal with the plagues created by some pathetic religious beliefs.

Scientific knowledge

Throughout my life the knowledge of the vastness of our universe around us was continually expanding. Then the awareness of the global disasters regularly terminating so many forms of lives at random on our planet caused me to ponder about the attention of our God on us. It was the increase in the scientific depth of our understanding about our own existence that started puzzling my mind about the God concept that was solely created by religious human minds. Strangely, my prayers to God continued in my head for four decades although my concept of God had been dwindling out. I could not stop going through the addictive prayers in my head. There was no harm in that situation, but I could no longer even imagine the nature or purpose of God. I could not see the natural disasters and the loss of lifeforms on our globe as being intentions of any God or any God allowing those disasters to occur.

Our planet Earth was housing a multitude of lifeforms that had originated in the universe several billion years ago and strangely, some are still with us. During the period of four billion years in our Milky Way galaxy there have been a series of disasters and creations of numerous lifeforms that had continually advanced or disappeared. Luckily, one stage resulted in the creation of us human beings. We share the planet with lots of many other lifeforms for which we should have the greatest respect. The atoms in our bodies have had life experiences in the bodies of other lifeforms.

An egg laid by a butterfly later comes out as a caterpillar which constructs a cocoon and locks itself into it. The caterpillar then has all its molecules converted into a new form of life and becomes a butterfly. I wonder if the butterfly and caterpillar could even recognise their relationship if they met the other. We humans became the leading life form on the planet, but we must not forget that we have been sharing atoms and even some genes with other lifeforms that have been alongside us on our planet. Amongst the various lifeforms, we are the only ones to be thinking about some state of existence after death, which was very difficult for me to understand. I cannot comprehend the notion of some form of an after-life existence for me. That stupidity is what had resulted in human minds to be creating imaginary concepts of God and some eternal after-life existence without a body, but some stupid, un-imaginable concept called a soul.

In the scientific field, there had been many discoveries during the last century, but there was one that stands out like a tower. Normally humans got energy from matter with the atoms or molecules ending up being rearranged and releasing some energy, like we do with burning wood or eating food and obtaining energy from it. Then, almost out of nowhere a single person blasted the world with a fantastic concept of our existence. He lifted human imagination into a totally new field. It was in 1905 that Albert Einstein had stated a theory on the relationship between the states of energy and matter. Einstein then came up with another concept, the General Relativity theory in 1916. Amazingly, matter can be taken out of its existence to leave behind in its place some new energy.

Einstein's theory states that:
$$E = mc^2$$
[E is energy, m is mass and c is the speed of light.]

A vast amount of energy can be produced by the destruction of a small mass of matter. That was a concept that had been unimaginable by any other human. Even more surprisingly, scientists managed to apply Einstein's theories to produce an atomic bomb with a massive explosion. It was during World War II that the Americans managed to create the first atomic bomb in 1945. My own existence had started during the starting year of that war and my life came very close to termination in the final year of that war. That was when the dhow in which we were sailing from Africa across the Indian ocean actually sank close to India. Later that year two atom bombs were used against the Japanese to end the war Although the atomic bombing killed a lot of people, it ended the war which would have resulted in even greater human losses from both sides over a long period. Fortunately, nuclear bombs have not been used again in any war. Instead, we now have the production of electrical energy from nuclear power stations that we even use in our homes. Strangely, most humans are unaware that all the energy that comes to us from the sun is created by nuclear explosions within the sun. Einstein who passed away in 1955 has left planet Earth with an unimaginable concept of a conversion of only little matter into tremendous energy.

After I had qualified as an engineer in the 1960's, I remember the debates between two theories on the state of our universe. There was a Steady State theory saying that the universe has always been in its current state and will remain there. The Big Bang theory stated that our universe emerged from an explosion and is expanding. Earlier discovery of the movement of stars in space had been made by Edwin Hubble and in 1965 other scientists discovered cosmic wave radiation from all directions in space. What these discoveries led to was realization of the expansion of the universe. The frequency of light shift indicated that almost all the galaxies were moving away from us and the fastest movement related to the galaxies furthest away. This evidence supported the big bang theory which states that the universe started as a big bang from nothing and now was in a state of expansion. Naturally, there was the puzzle about a big bang out of nothing, but there was no doubt about the current expansion of the universe. Even our brilliant scientists could not fathom that out. At that time, no human had managed to conceive that the formula created by Einstein to creating an atom bomb could also be used to solve the mystery of the creation of our universe.

We humans had no idea about the creation of our universe. We had no idea of what could be outside the universe. However, in our universe most of the galaxies are swirling around something that we cannot see and call them black holes. The holes are black because they are drawing in not only the matter around them but also the light energy. Light does not need matter to flow through, but it can be deflected by the vast gravitational fields produced by extremely heavy stars. Light can end up being absorbed back by a heavy star that hides the existence of itself from the rest of the universe. That is known as a black hole, where no star can be seen. Humans do not know what is in the black hole. That co-incites with the mystery of the appearance of our universe in a Big Bang.

Our existence

We are created by our parents in the mother's womb by combining the genes from both parents in two sets of chromosomes that form the first single cell that absorbs matter from the mother's body to continue multiplying and diverging into a vast number of cells. The growth of the cells of our bodies is based on the information in the genes and gives us different size, shape, colour, physical and mental capabilities. When a person dies, all the matter particles that made up every part of the body then continues to exist in other places or in other forms of life. Some bones of dead bodies may maintain their form of existence for a long time. The rest of the body, including the brain, decays back into molecules and atoms which will continue to exist and be any part of a new life on our planet. All the atoms in our current bodies may have been used before in other lifeforms and may have also been inside a dinosaur, a film star, a chicken, a honeybee or an ant. Our bodies have already been releasing atoms and molecules that can be used by any of the other lifeforms.

During my life as well as at the end of my life cycle, all my atoms and molecules will be used by numerous other lifeforms on my planet. I do not wish for any after-life existence for me as I will miss some friends and even some family members who will be in different heavens as they were born in different religions to mine. I will also miss the music that is created only by humans and I have been thoroughly enjoying during my life. As I will not miss anything if I do not exist after life, I have ticked the box for "no existence whatsoever" after my life termination.

The zero concept

What is the value of zero on its own? On its own zero is worthless and unimaginable. Together with another number, the zero can be used worldwide.in numerous fields. Zero on its own means nothing, but one-zero pounds is ten pounds or only two pounds if we were using binary counting. Zero allows counting to be done in binary, octal, hexadecimal or any other counting system. The zero lifted the world from all other systems for numbers. The Roman numerals have no zero and although they provided some other method of counting, they could not be used to do any calculations. Initially, the zero was created in the Middle East more than two thousand years ago using various sorts of symbols, but the public did not have a unified set of rules for mathematical use. That zero was a philosophical concept that failed to be used mathematically by the public. The humans who created the pyramids may well have been using the zero concept that no other people could fathom. Then after AD 600 the concept of zero was imagined and developed in India by astronomer Brahmagupta, solely for mathematical use. The zero was generated as a circle symbol using a set of rules in a counting system of ten that provided enormous mathematical use. It also allowed the use of negative numbers that had been unimaginable. That is when the concept started impacting itself on human life. The Indian zero system had been developed from the earlier Arab concept of counting that failed to be picked up by ordinary people. It was trading Arabs who later picked up the Indian zero system and passed it to Europe, which called it the Arab numeral. It was the use of the zero system that the Europeans then generated science concepts that enabled the human lives to be hugely advanced.

Initially, Europe had been locked in its vision of the Earth being the centre of the universe as well as being locked in the Roman numeral system of counting. They thought that all the bodies in the sky moved around our Earth. However, in the sixteenth century Copernicus created the basic solar system of planets rotating around the sun and the Earth being one of the planets. Then Galileo observed and produced a better version of our solar system but was punished by the Christian Church to withdraw his theory that was contrary to their religious belief of the Earth being the centre of the universe. When the notion of the zero was brought to Europe by the Arabs, there was immense European objection to the creation of something that was nothing, to be used for mathematical use. Only after the later acceptance of the zero in Europe that fantastic science concepts started getting generated. That was followed by all the people of on our globe and lifted the human lives.

With the zero, the numerical values could be raised to any value; the decimal system uses nine other numbers and the binary system uses only one other. The value of the numbers could be immensely increased and even be decreased by using them on the other side of a decimal point. The adoption of zero in the counting system exploded mathematical concepts. The formula that Einstein produced could not even have been conjured up without the zero concept. Our lives have advanced enormously in many fields by the zero concept that is used by our wonderful digital computers. However, we humans would still be around if our zero had never been conceived.

Charles Darwin had stumbled onto the recognition of the evolution of life in Galapagos Islands in 1839 but had restrained the publishing of his understanding of life evolution for fear of upsetting religious beliefs. It was in 1859 that he was triggered into publishing his book because a friend of his had also stumbled onto the recognition of evolution of life in the Far East. In those days, it was the religious concepts that controlled the behaviour of thinkers and scientists. The God concepts created in human minds only arose from their incomprehension of what humans could see and experience but could not fathom the natural forces that created them. Charles Darwin's book was called, On the Origin of Species because he dared not to state that even human lives were in the chain of animal lives.

Energy is the Real God

What and where is God?

The human search for God has been like a climb to a mountain peak. There are many people gently moving up at a peaceful pace. However, some people prefer to scramble up a crevasse. There have been conflicts between people on different selected routes as well those Some people are being pushed down by others into the crevasse. It is unimaginable that all people are attempting to reach the same peak. On our planet, we humans have produced many different concepts of God. In my search for God I had managed to reach the peak of the mountain, but there I could not see anything that was unusual. Only after I had returned from my climb did I realise that my God was solely in my mind. God to me is just like the human creation of the zero. After my death, both these concepts will also be dead. The reader may have been puzzled by the space in the paragraph. It was nothing, but it may have affected the reading. Similarly, God, that is nothing is only created in human minds and painfully affecting only the human lives. No other lifeform on our planet can ever be that stupid.

Only in human heads

It is us humans that have created the zero concept for which all humans accept a universal set of rules. Similarly, we humans need to have an acceptable God concept to have a universal set of rules for a single God for all of us. I see that our varying religious beliefs have different God concepts that are like people trying to use the zero concept within the Roman numeral system of counting. A zero cannot be fitted into the Roman numeral system. Also, a zero cannot be used in our meals or our taste of music. We can use the zero concept only in mathematical applications. The human concepts of

God do not have any universal rules and are dragged into all aspects of human lives.

I see that some human concepts of life are like fairy tales that are given to children. Fairy tales can be great for children, but I cannot imagine adults believing that the fairy tales could be of practical use in their adult lives. In the fairy tale of Red Riding Hood, a wolf had eaten the mother of the little girl and then lay in that bed, pretending to be the mother and was asking the little girl to come in so that it could even eat the girl. However, Red Riding Hood was saved by a forest keeper, who killed the wolf and recovered the mother that had been eaten by the wolf. In life, we would not expect a grown-up girl to be behaving like Red Riding Hood. However, some religious behaviours on our planet are no different than that of the Red Riding Hood fairy tale. Religious concepts lead some stupid adult humans into killing other humans because of their different concepts of God. That stupidity is only in human minds that are supposed to be the most intelligent.

We may be the most intelligent lifeform on the planet, but we are the ones that have become more lost in our lives than any other lifeform on Earth. I feel that it is time for humans to legislate, not only against religious violence, but also against religious interferences in people's normal lives. Our different religious beliefs are like our different tastes for music. People can produce and listen to their own music to their hearts content, providing they do not disturb their neighbours who have different taste of music. Just like I am happy with my music, I am happy with my God concept and I don't mind what God concept other people like to have, providing they don't disturb my life with their concept.

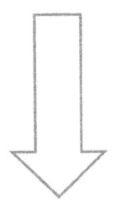

Energy is the Real God

> *It is only the human mind that has created the God concept.*
> *The God's intentions do not explain natural disasters on us.*
> *The God created by us does not use universal set of rules.*
> *Our God is what creates misery for innocent humans.*
> *We can only imagine a better life after death.*
> *There is nothing after life.*
> *Alas, God is nothing.*
> *A zero too is nothing.*
> *Zero is only in our heads.*
> *It is used without any conflicts in life.*
> *Zero uses a set of rules accepted by all humanity.*
> *Only we humans conceive a weird existence after life.*
> *After our life, there will be no Zero or human Soul or God.*
> *The God in human minds is not as good as our Zero concept.*

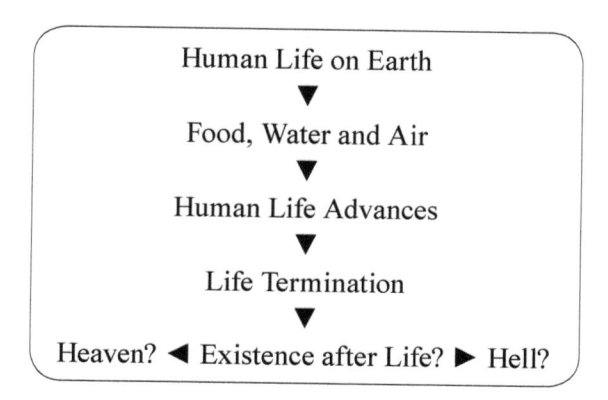

The human stupidity of an eternal life after death.

It was only the humans that created the different concepts of the religious beliefs called God. Is that God related to all life or only to human life? Why is the enormously vast space necessary for the most advanced form of life to exist only on a tiny speck in a vast universe? What is the purpose for such a big universe? What is the purpose for some state of existence after a life?

> Human Life on Earth
> ▼
> Food, Water and Air
> ▼
> Human Life Advances
> ▼
> Life Termination
> ▼
> Heaven? ◄ Existence after Life? ► Hell?

God and Nature

God had become a puzzle in my head. I finally found the solution when I replaced the word God with the word Nature which is the source of all the forces that result in the creations of matter, lifeforms and life delights as well as the disasters that we accept. In the old days, people used to sacrifice their children in response to the natural disasters occurring during their lives. I cannot understand the stupidity of any God creating disasters and sufferings for innocent humans and other life forms that are struggling for their survival. In replacing the word God with the word Nature, we humans could be curing our planet of the most pathetic human disease created by some religious beliefs that infect no other lifeforms on our planet. Religious humans have degraded themselves to *Homo Ignoramus*.

Energy is the Real God

Human life paths

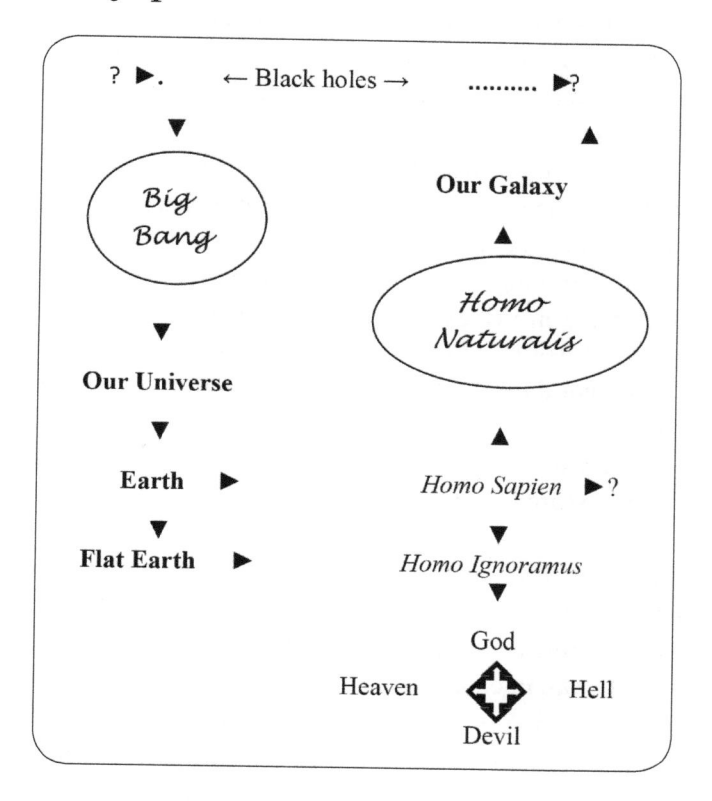

```
    ? ▶.        ← Black holes →      ......... ▶?
      ▼                                  ▲
   ( Big )                          Our Galaxy
   ( Bang )                              ▲
                                   ( Homo    )
      ▼                            ( Naturalis )
  Our Universe
      ▼                                  ▲
    Earth  ▶                      Homo Sapien ▶?
      ▼                                  ▼
  Flat Earth ▶                    Homo Ignoramus
                                         ▼
                                        God
                           Heaven  ✛  Hell
                                       Devil
```

Mystery of my own life

    I can see my small planet in the universe as being no more than a grain of sand on a beach. What lifted my existence in the universe was when I could see a beautiful light shining from sand on the beach. That was because my small planet in the universe was a like a diamond on a beach. My existence on my planet has been the most delightful existence that I can comprehend. Any existence after termination of life is inconceivable in my mind. God was only a concept created solely in human minds living on a flat Earth. No religious human can even imagine an existence without a body after their life. In human lives, there is not just one God, but totally different God concepts have resulted in human lives being unable to enjoy their once only rare existence with other humans and other rare lifeforms on a planet that is as rare as a diamond on a beach.

After I had sorted out my God problem I was hit by an even bigger problem. I could not conceive where 'I' was. It may be obvious that my thinking is in my brain that is in my head, but it has been impossible for me to even imagine where 'I' could be to enable me to control the thinking in my brain. It then dawned on me that the greatest mystery in my existence was the concept that was 'Me' and not God. When I see myself in a mirror, all I see is the front of my body and not the 'Me' that controls my thinking. All I can say to humans is not to our waste lives in our search for God when the biggest mystery in our lives is 'Us'. I felt that I need not have wasted my life in my search for God but to have sorted out what controls my own brain.

For a human birth, one cell from a mother and one from a father is sufficient for the creation of a new life. Rather than having been created by a weird God, our existence had resulted from a human coupling that was intended or unintended, desired or not desired, known or not known or an attempted abortion survival. The only concept that seems to be bothering us humans is the termination of our lives. That unwelcome termination made humans create concepts of various existences after life which do not bother any other lifeforms on any planet. For a solution to the puzzle of some existence after death, I stumbled onto a simple answer.

Can death be experienced during lifetime?

My existence is apparent to me when I am awake. However, my experiences of life when I am asleep are different. During my light sleep I have dreams that I do sometimes recall after I am awake. A dream occurs when the brain is trying to store the day's experiences in different parts of the brain. We humans will be having dreams that are related to our life experiences of the day or our thinking during that day. Every person's dreams will be occurring only in their head. During our light sleep we can have dreams which can be pleasant or frightening. Dreams in our sleep are not a reality of life. Similarly, I see that our concepts of heaven and hell are not a reality of life, but nothing more than dreams. However, in our deep sleep we do not have any dreams. We are in a state in which we do not have any conceptions. That state does not give us any pleasure or pain. I see deep sleep as being a state when I do not even exist. To me, my state of mind in a deep sleep is like me being in a state of death. It may seem simple, but that state of mind is what I feel I will have when I am not in existence. Strangely, during our lives, we humans all have several short experiences of death every day when we go into our deep sleep. I must admit that I had never imagined that I would ever be totally released from pondering about the mystery of some form of existence after death because I have already experienced it. Now my philosophy of life is simple.

Human God is nothing;
death is just like deep sleep.

Life delight

My life has been to me like the different experiences of day and night. During the day, I experience the joy of existence and during my sleep I am in a state of peaceful non-existence. Every day is a bonus existence for me. After my total non-existence, all atoms of my body will remain on my planet. My body could be cremated, and the ashes scattered into the sea or my body could be eaten by other lifeforms on my planet, just like what I have been doing during my life. Anyone looking for me after their own life termination will be wasting their time, whether they are going to be in Heaven or in Hell. After my life, I will not even be a zero.

We humans should be fascinated with our experience of a

wonderful existence on a multi-life planet in a vast universe. We should not be wasting time during our current existence by thinking about some stupid existence after our life is over. Earlier humans on a flat Earth were being mystified by lightning strikes from the sky and earthquakes from the ground. The understanding of our existence has advanced enormously to unravel the mystery of our existence inside our only universe.

God is nought
Just like our creation of the zero,
God is a human creation of a hero.
After life, with God I could be.
Nothing will we both see.
Aum

ॐ

2

UNBELIEVABLE ORIGIN OF LIFE

Creation of our universe

Our universe was created by a Big Bang. It was a flash that created space, matter and time. The period of 13.8 billion years is only applicable to life on planet Earth and not anywhere else in our universe. Later it was the human scientific minds that created the understanding that some energy in a pot had been through a strange process to appear as a universe in some space. The universe itself is created by energy. It was always energy that was the creator of matter and space. It was the matter together with energy that was converted to life. Without energy, there would be no space, no time, no light, no matter and no life.

The scientific concept of Einstein is the most unique concept in human minds. Strangely, even Einstein was unaware of the significance of his revelation to the humans. Initially, humans managed to create atom bomb using Einstein's formula. Then we managed to create peaceful power stations for electrical energy. To me, Einstein formula even explains the creation of our universe. Einstein's formula that stated:

$$E=mc^2$$
(E=energy, m= mass of matter and c=speed of light)

$(c^2 = 3x10^8 \times 3x\ 10^8 = 9 \times 10^{16} = 90\ quadrillion)$

The amazing atom particle

The matter in our universe is made up of the initial particle called the neutron that only responds to gravity. The creation of the atom is the most amazing change to the neutron because the small neutron is expanded by an injection of energy to become an enormous spherical shape while remaining at its original weight. That is like a small speck of rubber becoming an enormously vast balloon if it is inflated. As the energy does not have any weight at any time, the weight of the atom is the same as the neutron. During the inflation with energy, the neutron is transformed into becoming the atom that is made up of two new parts of matter.

Firstly, the heavy particle called proton is stationary at the centre of the atom and has at least 99.9 percent of the weight of the neutron. The other particle, the electron is orbiting around the proton, is extremely light in weight. It is ten thousand times lighter than the proton but has an equal and opposite charge of electricity. For the atom to maintain its existence, the tiny electron becomes the shell around the proton. It is energy that maintains the electron in a spherical orbit. Without the property of electrical charges, there would have been no atoms. Without the atoms, there would have been no lifeforms in the entire universe. The two particles that make up the first atom try to remain together for the whole period of existence in the universe.

Although, the proton/electron pair were created from a single neutron particle, they were flung apart by energy. The tiny neutron becomes million times bigger in size when it converts to becoming an atom. This will shock all humans to realise that our bodies are made of atoms which occupy so much space that we would not be visible or alive if we were not made up of atoms. On the other hand, even a tiny pebble from a star that is made up of neutrons only, will have enormous gravity on our planet. Humans should be careful about stepping onto a neutron star that will be the size of a planet and will not be shining out any light from itself. However, it's enormous gravity will only result in only an extremely short period of existence for the visitors who had decided to go touring around the universe.

Origin of human life

Earlier, humans only managed to create an imaginary God as the creator of life. Later, various human lives have not only conceived, but also discovered the universe. They even figured out the origin of the universe as well as the destination for our galaxy of stars. However, we humans have not managed to solve the problem of the origin of life. Was life only on the most amazing planet in the universe or were there other places where life may also have originated? Also, are any of those lifeforms still in existence or have they been exterminated?

We humans may currently be the most advanced life on our planet, but we are unaware of the origin of all the life around us. In reality, life had been in existence even before our planet was born. It was shortly after the birth of our universe that life had originated out of energy and matter. We humans may be the most advanced life form on Earth, but we are unaware of the original form of life. Most humans are also unaware of how or why our sun is sending out the energy necessary for the existence for all the lifeforms on earth. Without the continuous supply of energy by our sun there would be none of the advanced forms of life on any of our planets. It was the continuing process of evolution that had resulted in the later creation of the plant and the animal lives. The plant lives can obtain their energy from the sun whereas the animal lives need the energy initially gathered by the plants or by animals. We humans are unaware that we have to associate with other lifeforms in order to obtain the energy as we cannot obtain energy for our body cells directly from the sun. To provide ourselves with energy and to protect our own lives, our advanced intelligence requires us to associate with the other lifeforms in different ways for our own survival. That requires us to be aware of our role and purpose in a unique existence.

During my life, I had managed to recognise that I can control the thinking in my brain only when I am awake. I also recognise that death is no different to being in deep sleep. That simple realisation has also enabled me to solve the mystery of the origin of life. It was only an apple falling on the head of Isaac Newton that triggered the man to realise the reality of gravity. It had been fortunate that Newton was sitting under an apple tree and not a coconut tree. Without our knowledge of gravity, there would have been no creation of our universe. Similarly, something (not a coconut) has fallen on my head and I now wonder if I can wake up all human beings to make them understand the mystery of the origin of life in the entire universe. My concept of the origin of life will shock even the most scientific humans on my planet.

The atom is the origin of life. If not, then what is?

The existence of the atom is what has created the starting point of life in the entire universe. All matter in the universe had originated from energy that had first converted into being a neutron. After a short period, the neutrons absorbed further energy to become the atoms. The word atom was created by the Greeks who named it as the smallest particle of matter. Little did they realise that they had created a beautiful word for the first stage of life in our universe. Even scientists looking for some life on other planets are going to be astounded to find that the starting points of all life in the universe is in rocks and puddles of water beside them as well as in their bodies. We need to wake up to the reality of our existence and not waste our energy in a search for life elsewhere. There is hardly anywhere that we could go where there was no life. The only place in our universe for neutrons to be on their own, happens to be the neutron star that is not producing any light. Any human going to what looks like a planet will experience infinite gravity and termination of life.

Just like the concept created only by human minds called zero, the atom is only a concept that has been created by human minds to understand the creation of matter, the stars, the planets and human existence. Just like the zero, the atom makes good sense to human minds. The first atom to come into existence is the hydrogen atom and has been evolving into the other atoms in our universe. Despite that, the hydrogen atoms are still the major number of atoms in our entire universe. Being the lightest atom, hydrogen atoms are on the outer surfaces of all the stars in our universe. The light from all the stars is created by the process of hydrogen atoms being converted to heavier helium atoms by gravity. That results in energy being released as light. That is also what we humans can now be doing on Earth by exploding the hydrogen bombs. A bomb is nothing other than too much energy close to you.

All and every activity in any plant, animal and human lifeform is entirely based on the activity of atoms in the bodies. It had been the combinations of atoms that had created advanced lifeforms called molecules that then became associated with the creations of numerous advanced life organisms. The atom is the reality of not only the current life in the universe, but it also solves the problem of the disappearance of life from our universe, simply by transforming themselves back into energy via a black hole to return to their home, which is the dimensionless energy.

The creation, existence and termination of the universe had been solved by the advanced scientific humans. However, the starting point of life in the universe has remained to be a mystery that even scientific humans had been unable to solve. I wonder if I can wake up humans (including the scientists) to understand that the atoms are the origins of all life. That recognition should lift all human lives out of the trenches that they are digging with their ancient thinking. The following explanations of the simplified Einstein formula are there to help all religious humans as well as the scientific humans to wake up to the reality of life.

> The simplified Einstein formula is:
> $$E = m$$
> Enormous Energy = a little matter
>
> Energy and matter are interchangeable $E \leftrightarrow m$
>
> Human realisation is: **LIFE = E + m**
>
> Both matter and energy are necessary for the creation and existence of life.

Without energy or matter there is no life

Energy should be recognized by the humans to be, not only the creator of our universe, but also the participator in our lives. Humans who are aware of our universe also need to wake up to the fact that, initially all that was needed to create our universe, our matter and our lives was only energy. That recognition is all that is needed for humans to understand the existence of what we can see, use and participate with, for our existence in our universe. Our entire universe was not only created, but also maintained by energy, the real God. Just like an explanation for the existence of our universe was needed to lift earlier humans up from their existence on a flat earth, I now see that humans need to be educated about our existence in our galaxy. For the creation of a universe both energy and matter are required. Energy is the source of everything. Energy is the word that totally explains everything about our existence. The atom was created by energy. I was created by the atom together with energy. I now know that energy is the creator of both the atom and me.

Infinity, Eternity, God and Zero

We humans have words in our languages that are used to say something that we cannot imagine. Infinity is a number that has no end and cannot be conceived or used in mathematics. The word infinity was presented as the symbol, ∞ that will be placed by mathematicians when they cannot even conceive the end of a number. Similarly, the word eternity relates to the time period that does not have an end and is only used to state something that is inconceivable. God in religious heads is also only a vague human word to state something of which no human has any concept. Religious people have different concepts of gods which produces totally different behaviours from religious humans. On the other hand, the zero concept is the only human word that not only makes sense but is used by all humans on our planet without any objection, despite the fact, that the zero means nothing. That is because we have a set of rules for the use of that word only for specific applications.

Genetic life

It will surprise advanced human lives to being unaware of the fact that the numerous genes in our bodies still have the /codes of our earlier forms of life of being fish and animal lifeforms. The genes in our bodies are contained in the 23 pairs of chromosomes in most of the cells in our bodies. Each set of chromosomes are received from each parent. The genes are made up of 4 different bonds which are labelled as A. C. G and T. The fundamental point about life is that all these 4 bonds are made up of molecules which themselves made up of nothing other than the combinations of atoms. They reveal that the origins of all lifeforms in our entire universe are fundamentally created and maintained by the behaviours of the atoms in our universe.

The genes in our bodies should be recognized to be a lifeform that are solely interested in maintaining and advancing their own lives. Any baby of any form of life in space, in the air, in the sea or in the womb of a human, goes through those various earlier states of existence of atomic activities of their bodies. We humans, the supposedly most advanced state of existence on our planet are totally ignorant of the origin of any life on our planet and more importantly, the origin of our own life. It is only the human lives have created the stupid concept of some weird existence after death.

Locations of lifeforms

Just like human lives had advanced enormously after recognizing that the earth was a globe, now humans need to wake up to the fact that there is life in the entire universe. The creator of all lives in the universe is energy and nothing else. Energy not only created matter, but energy also feeds the matter. We humans should start recognizing that there is life in the entire universe where we exist. All humans who have been inspired to explore our planetary system for some other lifeforms need to think again. We do not even need to get up from our sofa to be able to see and touch other lifeforms that exist in the entire universe. Readers who may be shocked by this realisation are warned there are more kicks that they may experience to their minds if they read on in this book.

3

DIFFERENT FORMS OF LIFE ON EARTH

Our universe in sight

Our universe had been created, together with space and time, within energy. Our galaxy rotation situation is what a person could be seeing when sitting in a bath where the water that is covered by a layer of foam. Only a tiny bit of water together with a tiny bit of soap, traps numerous big bubbles of air to form a vast layer of foam. The head of the person is only seeing the large layer of foam floating on top of the massive quantity of water that is completely out of sight. That is similar to what we can see to be our universe, but we cannot imagine anything that is out of sight. A circle appearing in the layer of foam may alert the bather that the bath is draining. That is what we humans are seeing in our galaxies that are swirling. The black holes in the sky are like the out-of-sight drain hole in the bath that becomes unplugged. For even a bath that has been unplugged, it may be a while before the swirl will start to appear in the foam. The water in the foam is only a small quantity of the vast amount of water that fills the whole bath.

Similarly, all large enough galaxies will have black holes that are out of our sight or may be waiting to be formed. Also, we humans cannot comprehend the cause for the immense rate of expansion of the universe that we can see, because we cannot see aspects of the universe that are out of our sight. No person needs to jump into a rocket and go shooting out into space to look at the universe. Just have a relaxing hot bath.

Our universe has numerous galaxies that may or may not have any swirls at their centres. However, in the universe there are only few galaxies that are moving towards each other, like lovers do. The good news for the lives in the Milky Way galaxy is that our galaxy will not be going out of the universe on its own. Instead, our galaxy is going to be coupled by another galaxy that is two million light years away (it takes 2 million years for the light to travel) from us and is, strangely heading towards us. One day, the two mates will get close enough to start doing a circular dance together. Then, after a loving unison, the pair will dive down together into a black hole.

Some stars have small planets orbiting around those stars. The planets are nothing more than little specks of seed drifting away from a huge tree. Although we humans are thrilled with our existence on our planet, we have not been able to sight any other little planet that could be as lively as planet Earth. I wonder if a discovery of another similar planet will thrill us or disappoint us. Maybe, even the other lifeforms at another location could be disappointed with meeting us stupid humans. My existence in this universe is solely for the tiny grain of sand on a beach because, to me, my planet is like a diamond on a vast beach made up of sand. I do not need to go anywhere, as my life on earth could never be matched anywhere else. Only humans have some conception of a better existence somewhere else or some other time. I have decided to make the most of my life on my real planet than for imagining some other form of existence in some location where there are no bodies, but only invisible souls.

Humans who understand that the atom is the starting point of all life, will have no difficulty in recognizing that all the matter particles that make up a planet are all lifeforms in different states of their existences. For humans on spaceships landing on other planets, there would be no point in them stepping out to look for any lifeform if they had not been briefed before take-off to only look for some advanced life like moss, yeast or fungi. Maybe, some intelligent astronauts will return from a visit to another planet with life from that planet and baffle some ignorant scientists on Earth with packets of ordinary dust and rocks. We humans need to become aware of our own existence on the most beautiful location in the entire universe.

A star throws out energy and matter out of its body during its life. Initially, the humans could only detect the light energy being released by stars that are growing up. Only after our scientific advances, we were able to detect far more energy than what we can see that is released by the stars. We also detect some matter being ejected from stars. Human lives depend entirely on the energy released by one ordinary star in the Milky Way galaxy, our sun. We should recognise that the sun as our parent that is also getting older. During its aging process, it is also constantly throwing bundles of matter outwards from its equator.

During my visits to Norway, I had seen some particles of matter smashing into our upper atmosphere. Those were the *Aurora Borealis* green clouds swaying around in the night sky. However, I hope that no bundle of some heavy matter from our parent is going to fly out and smack us one day. We have no capability of predicting that event, but we will have realisation of that event only a short period before a massive impact on one side of our planet. One of the current emissions from the sun could turn out to be a rather large one, shooting out in the direction of our little planet. We can only hope that it does not happen in the next thousand years. For me, a century will be fine. We humans should be aware of the vastness of our universe. We should not be wasting our unique existence on a planet and go out, looking for some stupid existence on another globe.

Plant and animal lives

It was the birth of our universe that had resulted in the creations of the atoms, molecules, stars and planets. A few of the planets then evolved further to create lifeforms in the sea, on land and in the air. Plant lives had originated in the sea and floated in the water to gain energy from the sun or from volcanoes in the sea and particles of matter from the sea. The plant lives started evolving to seaweeds that did not need to spend any energy for movement because they were moved around by the sea tides. However, some plants even ended up being dumped on the shores by sea tides. On land, the plants lives could obtain the energy from the sun but needed water from the ground for them to survive. Eventually, some plant lives on land survived and evolved to become plants and trees at some fixed locations. The plants were the first advanced forms to start evolving further and occupying both the sea and the land on our wonderful planet.

The inability of some plants in the sea to trap any energy resulted in some plant lives starting to get energy from other plant lives. However, that resulted in those desperate lifeforms to move themselves around instead of being pushed around by the sea. That resulted in those lifeforms then evolving to become various sea animals that could survive by eating plant lives and getting some energy. Some of those animals even started eating other sea animals for obtaining more energy more easily. That was the birth of animal lives in the sea that evolved from the plant lives simply to obtain some energy for their new existence. Animal lives could not do what the plant lives could, that is, obtain energy directly from the sun. Later, the animal lives in the sea transferred to land as well in order to eat the plant lives initially and later into eating other animal lives. Plant, animal and insect lives are the advanced stages of evolutions of lives in the sea and on land.

Creation of sex lives

The most amazing path in the evolution of life on our planet was the creation of the sex life among numerous plants, animals and insects in the sea as well as on land. Sex lives have two different sets of genes in their bodies that would integrate into a better combination for survival and progress of those lives. With the enormous changes in the environments occurring on the globe, a lot of the non-sexual lives on our planet were struggling to survive, but the sexual lives survived those circumstances because of their modified bodies. Later, the creation of the sex life resulted in an advantage for survival as well as better progress.

Sea plants and animals were later pushed out of the water or were prompted to move to land. Evolutions of life on Earth have resulted in the creations of enormously large forms of life on land. Some of the land creatures started even moving through the air by flying. It is amazing all these activities in the sea, land and air are nothing more than the life activities of the atoms that became engaged in actions purely because of injections of energy into the atoms. The only period of rest that occurs during the lives of the atoms is when they ae not being disturbed by any energy or electrons from other atoms.

The sexual creatures on our planet evolved rapidly to become higher forms of life, which may or may not have occurred on other planets. The evolutionary processes and sexual lives of the animals, insects and plants have mainly been advancing the lives on our planet to maintain their existences. However, some very ancient lifeforms are still with us after having survived from all the disasters that have been affecting our planet. We humans are only recent creatures on planet Earth and are still in our evolutionary progress. Human lives had been triggered into using only two of the limbs for moving around. That resulted in using the two spare limbs for totally different uses and became the stimulus for advances in those lives. Humans are the only mammals that only use a pair of legs for walking. The monkey and the ape species use their arms for both walking as well as for handling. Humans, on the other hand can use their arms for anything else at any time or walk around with their hands in their trouser pockets. That situation had arisen from the humans that needed to hold the head high for sighting around in high grass in Africa. Later, the uses of the human arms, hands and grips resulted in the humans evolving to the highest state of intelligence amongst all the other lifeforms on our planet. However, it has also resulted in creating some real problems in human lives.

Amongst the mammals there are others that use their front limbs for gripping, fighting or moving. None of those activities are anything as complex as what the humans can indulge in with their hands. Amongst the dinosaur species of animal lives, the breed that had survived were the ones that had started using the forward pair of limbs for flying. However, that did not advance those lives like the human lives have achieved. Due to the evolutionary advance of human lives the movement of the legs required the repositioning of the limbs and some organs inside their bodies. That also resulted in some changes to the sex lives of the mammals for the delivery of the babies out of wombs at an earlier age. That is why human and ape children are born earlier and need to be handled for feeding and movement. The four-legged mammals have no problems with the delivery or handing the babies. A new-born antelope, deer, zebra or lion will have no problem with getting up and drinking some milk themselves. No human baby could ever manage to do that. The most advanced lifeforms have more problems with raising children than any other mammals. The more advanced the lifeform, the more complex becomes the creation and the upbringing of the children. That has resulted in the weirdest problem for the most advanced life form on the most wonderful planet.

The two-legged status of existence occurred in the human lives only recently when compared to the evolutions of other forms of life on our planet. The huge dinosaurs had evolved into flying species that converted the use one pair of limbs for flying and the other for walking when on the ground. After the major disaster sixty-five million ago the flying dinosaurs are those that survived and evolved into smaller forms of life called birds. The birds had started having the same problem that we humans are having during our extremely short period of existence. Our problem was the inability of being able to smell the sexual readiness of the females for creation of new lives. Instead of using smell, the birds developed a process in which the males created visible or aural attractions for any female that was ready for sexual activity. The males started using their abilities to produce sound or dance with colourful feathers to attract the females and to repel other males. The courtship activities of the male birds are a delightful activity for us humans to watch.

The free use of hands in the human lives resulted in us humans leaping forward that no other lifeform had been capable of. However, we humans have had little time in which some fundamental change that needs to be incorporated into our lives to replace the inability of the males to smell the sexual readiness of the females for sexual activity for life creation, that the mammals are doing without any problems. We are the only lifeforms that are engaging in sexual activity with no intention or desire for the creation of a life. Most humans do not even recognise that human problem. No one has ever suggested a solution.

4

PLAGUES CREATED BY HUMANS

Human sex life

The human sexual life did not advance in pace with changes of the body necessary for adapting to the two-legged posture. The creation of that posture resulted in the noses of the males to move away from the position where it could smell the sexual readiness of the female for sex. The rate of human mental development is enormously faster than the rest of the body changes necessary for the new state of existence. Hardly any human has recognized that the sexual lives of the humans are totally unnatural, compared to all the other lifeforms on our planet. That situation may not have been noticed by humans because, being the most superior lifeform, we humans could not even imagine that human sexual life could be unnatural. We humans need to recognise that only we humans are affected by that sexual problem. It was only after my recognition of the problem that I understood the cause of that problem.

It is embarrassing to reveal to humans that the posture that had resulted in us rising to be the most intelligent lifeform on our planet, had also resulted in the most unnatural sexual life on our planet. Our sexual problem was created solely by the two-legged posture of our bodies. That problem was created by the fact that the human noses were no longer at the same level as the sexual organs. We humans can recognise the need for that situation when we see the male dogs will regularly be sniffing the sexual organ of the female dogs to detect the readiness of the female for some sexual intercourse for the creation of a new life, although they may not be aware of that fact. No sexual activity will take place if the female is not ready and nor will there be any attempt by the male dog to force a sexual engagement. No humans are offended by dogs engaging in sexual activities. However, we humans do not have the ability to detect the sexual readiness of the females to engage in the sexual activity because of the noses of the males is no longer at the position of the female organs.

The human inability to smell the sexual readiness of the females resulted in the sexual lives of the humans taking a totally unnatural approach. It was the human females that started to signal to the males by using perfume smells to attract the males. That turns out to be totally opposite to the approaches for sexual activities in other two-legged animal lives that cannot smell the sexual readiness of the females, where normally it is the males that are singing, dancing or posturing to attract the females who may be ready for sex. The loss of the human male ability to sense the female sexual smell has changed the human sexual lives. No human male will now react normally to the natural smell of the female who is ready for sexual activity. What is more unusual is that human sexual activity is not for the creation of a new life.

During our childhood periods, the sexual organs are only used to pass out wastewater. Later, the sexual organs of the youngsters start to grow for their ability to create new lives. In the female bodies, the breasts start to grow out. In the male bodies, the testicles move out of the bodies. People carrying youngsters on the shoulders will have different impacts on the bodies of the children when they get older. The boys could be feeling pains when sitting on adult shoulders while the girls may be feeling some pleasure. That is why young females enjoying riding on horses across the back of the horse. In the past, women would be made to sit on a horse with both their legs to one side of the horse. Those strange encounters in human lives were only created by the situation of the humans starting to walk with only two legs. That resulted the human sexual organs ended up being placed in very unnatural positions. We humans have not had sufficient time during our recent existence to have evolved into adjusting our sexual activity while the human brain enabled us to even start interfering with the natural forces on our planet. The long living dinosaurs were the ones that had evolved to go flying. Their lives had also resulted in the birds having to evolve further to adjust their sexual activity. Instead of smelling the female readiness for sexual activity, the males resulted in singing, dancing and having colourful feathers for attracting the females.

Although human lives had resulted in advancing enormously at a rapid rate, we humans have also totally failed to notice that the human sexual was totally unnatural. All other animal and insect lifeforms on our planet have natural sexual behaviours. What is more surprising is that we humans have even not recognized the unnaturalness of our own sexual behaviour. During the early days of the human social gatherings, the males and females started dancing together without getting too close to each other. Later, the human pairs started to unite their bodies for the dancing. Some animals will also unite together, but that will be solely to engage in a sexual activity for the creation of a new life. The human sexual behaviours, on the other hand, are nothing to do with life creations. Only we humans have evolved into becoming the most unnatural sexual lives on a wonderful planet in the entire universe.

The current sexual lives of the humans are still in the status on being totally unnatural and we humans need to recognise that before we can even start thinking about finding a solution for curing the disease that is only in the human bodies. My revelation will be shocking human minds, but it is only the human minds that could create some treatment for that disease. We humans may be the most intelligent lifeforms of a planet, but we also need to be alerted to the fact that our life is the only life on Earth that is in the process of extinguishing itself in a very short period of existence. We humans are the only life on our planet that is creating or stupidly accepting the most unnatural path of life. All other lifeforms have sexual behaviours solely for the creations of life. We humans are transforming the natural process of creations of life into a totally unnatural process. No other lifeform on Earth is that stupid even though some animal lives may even engage into life terminations of other lives (mainly males) just to create children of their own.

We humans, on the other hand, are having sexual activity solely for pleasure when the sole natural purpose had been for the creations of life. Only humans have ditched the natural function of creating new lives. Even amongst the normal human families, the number of sexual engagements relating to the creations of new lives is totally unnatural. Some humans do not even wish to produce children but will engage in sexual activity with same sex humans or animals or children or dummies. Only humans are killing the children in their wombs that they had unintentionally created. Only we humans turn out to be the most stupid lifeform on our wonderful planet. What on Earth can solve the problem that is only created by human lives?

Firstly, we humans need to be aware that our own lives are the most unnatural sexual life on the most wonderful planet in the universe. It is the adults that need to be educated. Secondly, education of the natural function of sex should start being taught early to children at an early age and continued in their later education, with the stress that sex is for the natural creation of a life. If the children are not alerted, then there will be little chance of influencing them when they are older and start to experience the pleasure of sexual ejection or massage. The chance of totally wiping out the unnatural sexual activity of the two-legged creatures is going to be very difficult to solve. The only solution for the human sexual problem will be revealed in a later chapter.

Money

When money had initially been created, it had been serving the early humans well, to integrate into larger groups and activities. During the initial stages of usage of money, the amount of money earned by humans was related to the usefulness of their ability to help other humans for their survival or for gaining the ability to improve their existence. Now, we humans have become the only lifeform on our planet that solely relies on money for our survival because the natural processes of survival have been totally flushed out of human minds. Without instant access to food, most humans will have less chance of survival than the ants, the birds, the bees and antelopes. With lives controlled by money, the natural ability for life survival has become totally unnatural amongst the supposedly most intelligent forms of life on a planet.

All the nations on the planets have become entrenched into the same ditch because nations now use their money to trade with other nations and the whole planet is suffering from the same plague. It is time that humans start to recognise that money is something that had been created only by the human minds. Humans need to be alerted to the fact that an artificial creation by human minds will never be the joy of our existence on a unique planet. We humans must try to associate our lives with the numerous natural lifeforms here. That requires us to start disassociating our lives with money, the artificiality created by us.

Ownership of land

The human life is the only form of life on a planet that has created the stupidity called individual ownership relating to the land on which they are living on. A plot of land on a planet can be owned forever by a human individual because only we humans have created that stupidity. However, only some sensible humans managed to establish some rules for. the areas of the seas, the regions of ice and land around the north and south poles, the earth deep below and the space above their plot of land that cannot be owned by any human for any period. They also decided not to allow any human to own anything on the moon, the planets or any space rock. Only we humans have created global stupidities.

All the other lifeforms on our planet go and find locations in the seas, the land and the air for their survival. They have all evolved to fit in with their environments on the planet that they are all sharing with the others. The energy required by them is mostly provided by the bodies of other lifeforms. Some animal lives make do with vegetarian food like fruit, seed or leaves provided by the plant lives. On the other hand, almost all the plant lives maintain their existence and survival solely by using the energy from the sun. They do not threaten any animal lives but will compete with other plant lives for space to maintain their access to the sunlight. In fact, plant lives provide fruit to vegetarian animal lives to prevent termination of their own lives as well as to enable the spread of their seeds to wider locations.

Climate change

Burning the remains of the plants after their life cycles provided us humans with energy for various purposes. The initial process of burning has enabled humans to advance their lives above all other lifeforms. Currently, we humans are the ones that are also triggering a rapid change in our global climate. We humans are turning out to be the most polluting species on a unique planet that are triggering rapid environmental changes. The human extractions of oil and gas from the solid surface of a planet are interfering in the natural life cycles of numerous plants on earth and some lives below the sea.

Earlier, humans had even not been aware the pollutions that those exhausts were creating, because the countries suffering from the pollutions were not the ones that were burning those fuels. It is time that we humans start to recognise that the planet on which we are living is the only planet for any of us. The plentiful burning of oil and gas by humans is creating immensely polluting exhausts around the whole planet. However, human usage of fuel for energy has grown so enormously that we humans are now triggering the process for life terminations for numerous lifeforms on our planet. We are also placing ourselves on that path where we are making the polar ice to rapidly change to water that will be flooding the coasts around the globe. There appears to be no vision of the path of human lives on a unique planet. Even our creation of the institution called the United Nations is unable to guide or control the pollution activities of human lives.

Human plagues being inhibited by coronavirus in 2020

It is the elementary species of life, called the coronavirus that is now inhibiting us humans who have been creating a very unnatural environment for our planet. We have been polluting the planet with our technology and artificial creations that are destroying the natural lives of the plants, animals and insects at an accelerated rate. To become a useful species of life, we humans need to have respect for the natural lives on our planet. Otherwise, the human lives will deserve to be exterminated by other lives, like the coronavirus. Thankfully, it is the coronavirus that is reducing the pathetic plagues of pollution that we humans have been inflicting on our whole planet with vehicles using oil, petrol and gas.

5

MYSTERIES OF HUMAN SPORTS

The lives of many modern humans are being channelled mainly by sports activities. As numerous humans are now engaged in watching sporting events in the stadiums or on television screens, the amount of money earned by sportsmen and sportswomen is so enormous that it vastly exceeds salaries associated with almost all other life activities including the members of governments. That is because normal humans are even prepared to spend lots of money to see sporting events. Life engagements with sports is now definitely, very much part of human lives around the globe. What amazes me is that even people playing some sport brilliantly do not have any idea of the origin of sports.

Only we humans have created our sporting activities and only we humans have created the money that we use. Now money and sports have also become linked closely. Sports is also affecting the lives of people living in countries that have totally different amounts of money than the other countries. Now, the money earned by some young sportsmen around the globe are even more than the people who are governing their nations. Sports turns out to be a big mystery of human behaviours. Surprisingly, most humans who are participating in sports or those who are paying to see the sporting activities around the planet have no idea about the origin of our sports.

For most of the other lifeforms on our planet, the preparation for adulthood requires the young ones to be indulging with playing activities in order to enable them to become capable of hunting for their food or for escaping from other lifeforms that are looking to eat them. As soon as the animals reach adulthood, then their childish sporting activities become real-life activities for their life survival or food for their bodies. We humans fail to recognise that the sportive activities that we engage in during our adulthood are nothing other what young children should have been doing to enable them to engage in real fighting when they grow up. However, human lives evolved into not needing to fight for survival or for food. That resulted in adult humans failing to detach themselves from the childhood activity of practicing to fight. Human adults continue with their childhood activity of fighting, but not killing. That activity has become their careers.

During my earlier life, I had been engaging in activities associated with nuclear attacks on the Soviet Union, if that war was ever to be triggered. As it turned out, we were never going to be engaged in that situation, because there would have been no winner. Now, I see that all human sports are doing that. By attacking others, without any killings, humans are achieving a superiority over the others in sporting events. That is why sporting events are turning out to be the biggest achievement as well as a source of income in many human lives. That situation seems to be affecting the national behaviours of countries around our globe.

However, sports also did not stop people from cheating. Now, the humans need to be checked for their sexual status before participation. We humans may be the most superior lifeforms, but we still could be using our brains to cheat the others. That situation is strangely associated with the body posture that the humans have acquired during our evolution.

The Olympics

The Olympic Games are the most amazing integration of human lives. That is where humans from all nations on our planet can compete with others and try to establish their superiority without engaging in any life terminations. The name of the games is based on the ancient human activities at a place in current Greece that is called Olympia that had open plains for large human gatherings. The initial games were started in 776 BC and held every four years for more than a thousand years. The ancient Olympics were abolished because the Romans had conquered that area and had adopted Christianity as their prime purpose of existence. They considered the Olympic contests to be pagan cults. Humans around the globe had been thrilled by the ancient Olympics and the decided to revive the human ability to try and integrate our lives on our planet. The modern Olympics started in 1896 in Athens and have continued to take place every four years after that, except for the world war interceptions.

The ancient Olympics had been the most amazing integration of different human lives in areas close to others. The inhabitants of the different areas would be informed about the start of the next Olympic and demanded to stop any fighting before, during or after the games. The games were to be treated as an opportunity for young men to demonstrate their physical qualities for fighting and establish their superiority amongst the neighbours. The games allowed the athletes and their families and friends from all regions to attend the games in safety. The athletes had to be males and of Greek origin. To prevent any females engaging in the games, all the competitors had to participate with naked bodies. No married women could come to the games, but unmarried women could watch the games.

All the games were for individuals competing against the others in competitions of physical abilities that are required to engage in fighting. That resulted in the athletes running, wrestling, boxing, martial art of boxing and wrestling, horse and chariot racing, as well as the pentathlon of running, long jump, discus, javelin and boxing.

Not many people recognise that all sports in modern human lives are related to humans demonstrating to be able to do some fighting. In each of the ancient games, there would be only one winner who would be presented with a palm leaf and a ribbon tied to his head as a sign of victory. However, at the end of the games there would be a presentation of a prize for a single overall winner of all the games who would have a crown made of olive branch on his head. That athlete would be welcomed as a hero back at his hometown.

The ancient activities of some humans on our planet are certainly helping us to recognise the need to integrate our lives for our survival. The ancient Greeks had created the Olympics to integrate those people. In effect, the modern Olympics is also trying to do that in uniting the humans on a globe. Now we are even including in our Olympics an event that occurred in Greece in 490 BC. After the Battle of Marathon, a Greek soldier took the message of the victory to Athens by running 26 miles and 385 yards. On arriving at Athens, the soldier presented the message, saying "We have won", then collapsing and dying. In 1986, other forms of life on our unique planet, the modern Olympics started using that episode to create the marathon run that is not only in the Olympics, but also in cities around the globe for masses of ordinary people as well as global athletes. I think that we humans should recognise that our natural stimulus for fighting should be directed mainly for sporting activities.

6
CREATION, EVOLUTION AND TERMINATION OF LIFE

Human lives being guided by computing systems

When I had been qualifying as an electrical engineer in the early 1960s, we were introduced to an advanced state of human invention called the transistor that was going to replace the electronic valves. During my flying in the Royal Air force during the 1960-1979 period, we used basic equipment with no computing technology. In the 1980s when I was lecturer, I had to become familiar with the electronic chips that were creating the start of microelectronics.

During the years of the 2000s the electronic computing has been transforming the paths of human lives. Humans are no longer on the natural path of life that all other ancient lifeforms on our planet are still following. We have now advanced to a state where we can already modify the life patterns of other lives on our planet as well as our own lives. We can also create new lives on our planet. All these advances had been triggered by the necessity to treat humans suffering from infection or genetic problems. Some of the new human discoveries are hidden from others for the simple reason that we humans have already reached the state of being able to interfere with the natural evolution of even our own lives on our planet.

Human sexual life problem

During the initial stages of plant and animal lives on Earth there was no sex. Only after a chance encounter of two lifeforms being united and inseparable, the sexual life advanced to a state of existence for both plants and animals. Although we humans may be the most advanced state of existence on our planet, we are now also the most degraded sexual life on earth.

The human lives are, not only the ones that have sexual activity solely for pleasure, but also the only ones that do not even desire to create new lives or will even abort the lives that they have created. We humans may be the most advanced lifeforms on this planet, but we also seem to be turning out to be the weirdest species of life. That is why the replacement of humans by a new form of life will be the best treatment for the cure of plagues that are solely created by us.

Homo non-sexual robotic

We humans are now capable of creating new forms of life as well as resurrecting the earlier extinguished lifeforms from the preserved parts of their bodies found in frozen ground. We are also capable of modifying the genes in our own bodies. I see humans walking past me and seem to be totally controlled by a hand computer with the headphones that are plugged into their ears. The future humans will not even need the earplugs, because their brains will be plugged to their control centre by a wireless connection. Although the human could be selecting whatever program it wishes to be engaged in, it would be totally controlled by massive computer control centres that. will be controlling the numerous robots that will be serving the computers as well as the homo sapiens. Modern homo sapiens themselves will start becoming the homo robotic. As robots do not actually have, nor do they need to have any sexual engagements, the homo sapiens will also themselves become the homo non-sexual robotic creatures. Their sexual genes will be extracted from their chromosomes. Every human brain will be linked to and will be served and controlled by the computing control centres. The reproduction of homo non-sexual robotic species will be created outside their bodies in centres that will further replace some of their genes with genes from other human bodies as well as from other lifeforms for the creation of a new non-sexual babies in laboratories and not in humans who will have no wombs. No human will ever be suffering from the process of creating a new life in their bodies. In the later system they could be having the pleasure of being presented with a baby that had been created in the laboratory to their own specification. That will be similar to the bodies of human babies being flown into their houses by the flying storks. The degrading sexual behaviour of human bodies will never be on our planet again.

Terminations of plant and animal lives

Plant lives on our planet obtain energy from the sun for their existence and survival. However, animal lifeforms obtain energy by either eating the plants or other animals. These situations have been created only by nature. However, if there is a change in the natural environment, then there will also be a change to the lives of both the plants and the animals. That is what will happen to all the plant and animal lives on our planet when the climate and environment will change dramatically. One day, the sun will have reached an old age when it will explode and extinguish itself as well as the advanced states of existences on its planets. However, the atomic lives will still be there, and they will later be having another dramatic change to their existence.

Emigration of all atoms to the pot of energy

The black hole of our galaxy will be at such great gravity, that all the atoms will collapse and become very small neutrons with the same weights. The Milky Way galaxy will then be stepping into a totally new existence. However, it is likely that our galaxy will unite with the Andromeda galaxy before embarking on a journey to take them back to the pot of energy from where they had originated. Every atom will transform itself into energy. Although, billions of atoms have been part of our delightful lives, we will never be anywhere, anytime ever again. All the atoms that had created us will be transformed back to energy in the pot of energy from where they had come. That is like what a molecule of water will be doing. From the ocean, the molecule could become a vapour, float up to become part of a cloud, an ice crystal, a drop of water to rain down to land and go through numerous stages of existence as ice on a mountain top, glacier, raging river, waterfall, calm stream, garden, plant life, animal life, insect life, human life, cremation and so on until finally it back into the ocean that it came from. That is what all the atoms in my body have been doing. Every atom in my body had come from the pot of energy and that is where every one of those atoms will be returning to. I hope that I could alert human lives that the atom is the origin of all life in our universe. It is Energy that is the sole creator, preserver and terminator of the atomic lives in our universe.

Our universe in sight

Our universe had been created, together with space and time, within a womb of energy. What we can see and detect is like what we humans see at the top of a hot bath that has a layer of foam created by a very small amount of the water and a little soap. However, when the bath plug is removed there is initially no sign of the drainage of water that is taking place. Later, the boundary of the layered surface will start to shrink, and a circular shape starts to appear to indicate the drain hole. Similarly, our Milky Way galaxy is like numerous other galaxies that are displaying their circular activity. However, even the galaxies without any circular drainage sign are like the bath that does not indicate drainage until the bath level reaches a lower level. We humans need to wake up to the fact that our circulating galaxy has a drain hole in place. The vast amount of energy that is part of our galaxy is like the vast amount of water that is out of our sight in a bathtub that has a layer of foam on top that is made up with only a small amount of water. The part of our galaxy in sight is like us sighting only the foam layer on the top of the vast amount of invisible water in the bathtub.

Just like the water in the bathtub coming out a tap ends up filling the bathtub, the Big Bang is the opening up of our universe being filled up with matter. Just like all the water in a bathtub will be disappearing out of the bathtub into a hole, so also galaxies in our universe have already disappeared and so will the Milky Way galaxy will be doing that. Just like all the water in every home had originally come out of the sea via the sky as cloud, dropped down to land as water or snow, flowed as rivers through land and fields and homes to go back to the sea, so also does the matter in our universe goes through its life experiences and finally goes, via the black holes in our universe, back to Energy, the Creator.

Rajinder Sharma

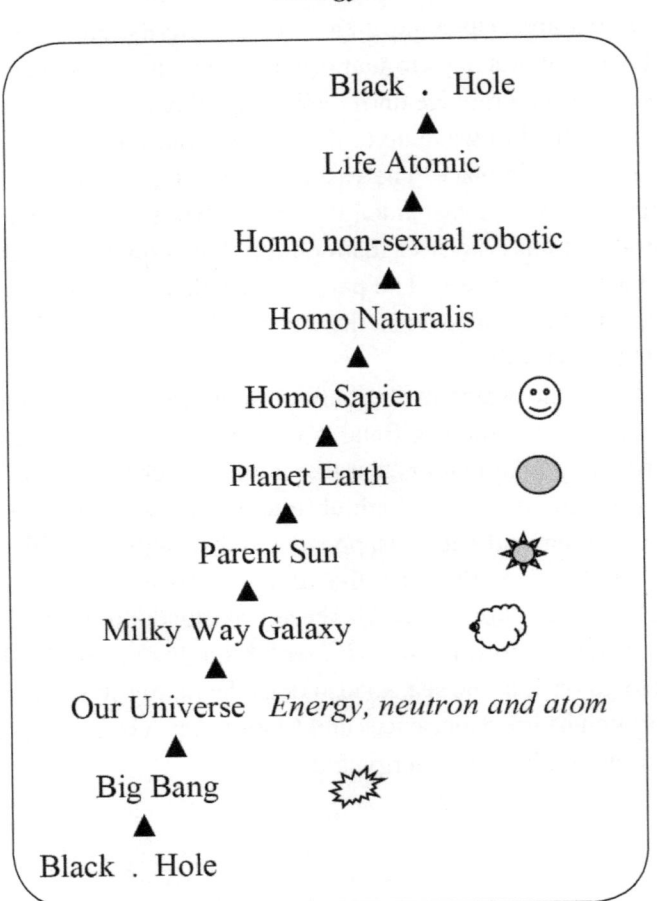

Energy

Black . Hole
▲
Life Atomic
▲
Homo non-sexual robotic
▲
Homo Naturalis
▲
Homo Sapien   ☺
▲
Planet Earth   ●
▲
Parent Sun   ☀
▲
Milky Way Galaxy   ☁
▲
Our Universe   *Energy, neutron and atom*
▲
Big Bang   ✸
▲
Black . Hole

Energy

7

THE SCIENTIFIC GOD

The scientific God is a reality

We had come into existence on a planet that seems to be no more than a speck of dust beside a grain of sand on a beach. Uniquely, a speck of dust turned out to be a shining diamond on a beach. Planet Earth came into existence 4.5 billion years ago in a universe that had come into existence 13.8 billion years ago. Energy is the creator of both matter and life in our universe. Energy is the participator in the activities of lifeforms in our entire universe. It is the black holes in our universe that have been and will continue transforming lifeforms back into matter and then transforming the matter to energy before returning the energy back into a dimensionless existence.

Space, time, matter and life in our universe had been created by energy. All the galaxies in our universe will return to the energy from which they had come.

Beyond our universe

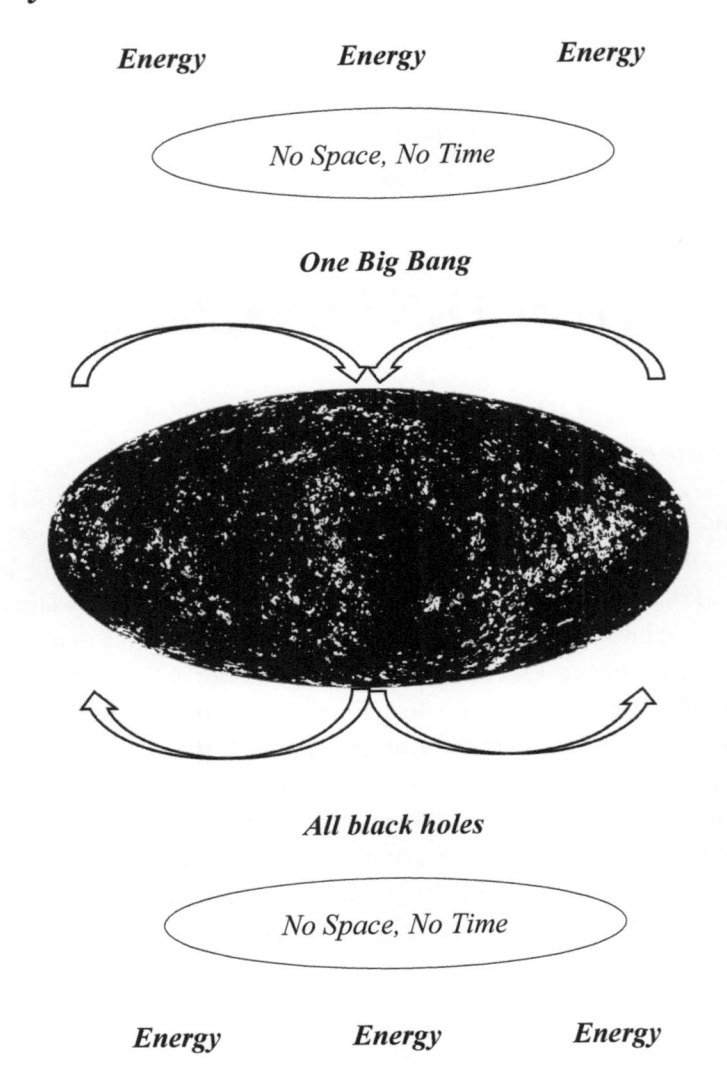

Energy *Energy* *Energy*

No Space, No Time

One Big Bang

All black holes

No Space, No Time

Energy *Energy* *Energy*

Energy in the bodies of lifeforms

Energy has been the creator of all the atoms and the bodies of all lifeforms that are entirely made up of the atoms. All the activity of the human bodies is associated with the input of energy that is released by the atoms in the Sun that is only a star. All the stars in the universe are in the process of an existence during which they evolve the hydrogen atoms into the creation of the advanced atoms that are heavier. The stars and planets have been going through some life and will finally reach the destination, which is the location of their origin, namely Energy. It was Energy that had created matter, space and time to create life in the entire universe. It is Energy that will take back what it had created in stages. Energy is the entity which has no need for space or for time.

We humans on a beautiful planet may be the most advanced form of life, but we are also the most unnatural ones. Infinity and eternity are fictious words that religious as well as scientific people have created to create some weird existence after life termination. The human brains are now in the process of destroying numerous natural lives as well as extinguishing our own advanced existence on a unique planet. There are many unnatural aspects of human lives that are polluting our beautiful planet. The main cause of the human problem is that we humans are unable to control our own brains to be serving our own bodies. The human brain in only a part of the body that is supposed to be looking after the body. The human brains should be controlled by the human minds, which modern humans have totally failed to recognise.

Human brain, mind, soul and God

The brain in a body of any lifeform is primarily for helping the body to survive, to feed and to create a new life for maintaining its existence on a unique planet. The human brain is a reality. Although the brain will continue looking after the body during its deep sleep or unconsciousness or been anaesthetised, that brain activity will not happen when a person is dead. However, during the unconsciousness period as well as after death, no person will ever experience any passage of time. During the process of dreaming we humans have the weird experiences that do not make sense. The human minds cannot control the dream experiences during the dreams. During deep sleep we do not have any dreams. That is when the human brain looks after the body.

The human mind, on the other hand, is something that can control the thinking within the brain with or without any physical activity. The human mind is both a reality and a mystery. The mind in a human brain will only function when the person is awake. During our state of dreaming or meditating there is a possibility that the mind could become some reality. However, when the human is in deep sleep, the mind does not function but the brain continues to be looking after the body. The minds in our bodies only exist when we are fully awake. When the body is dead, the mind can never, ever be in existence.

The soul is a creation only in human minds in the bodies that are not dead. A soul is a totally inexplicable concept that is totally different in different religious beliefs. The soul has no parts of the human body and cannot even be in sight of any other soul. No person with that pathetic thought has any explanation for the real meaning of the word. Souls and religious gods are nothing other than total unrealities only in the heads of humans living on a flat earth. On the other hand, Energy is the scientific God. Energy is the reality that creates the universe with the entities of space and time that are essential for life. Outside the universe there is no space and no time but only Energy, the real God.

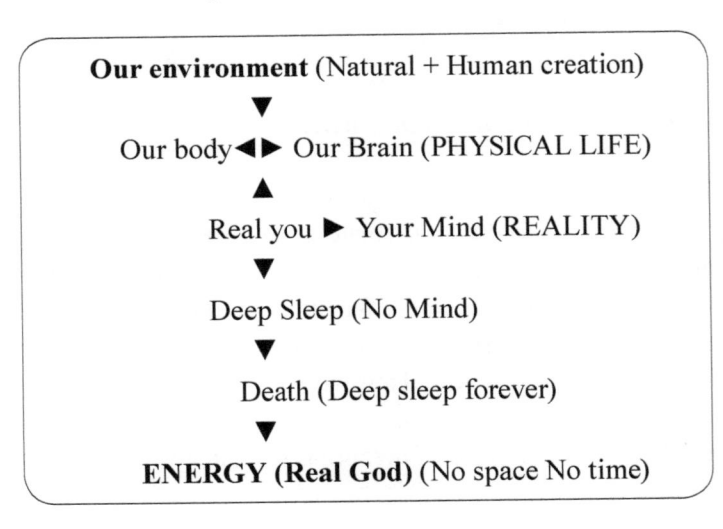

Our environment (Natural + Human creation)
▼
Our body ◄► Our Brain (PHYSICAL LIFE)
▲
Real you ► Your Mind (REALITY)
▼
Deep Sleep (No Mind)
▼
Death (Deep sleep forever)
▼
ENERGY (Real God) (No space No time)

Energy is the Real God

    Every human body is a unique combination of atomic lives to create a once-only existence. The termination of a human life does not result in the termination of any of the numerous atomic lives that had been in the body during that life. The atomic lives have been in existence for billions of years and will last for more billions of years.

    (A human year is only on our planet earth.)

Our life cycle with Energy, the Creator

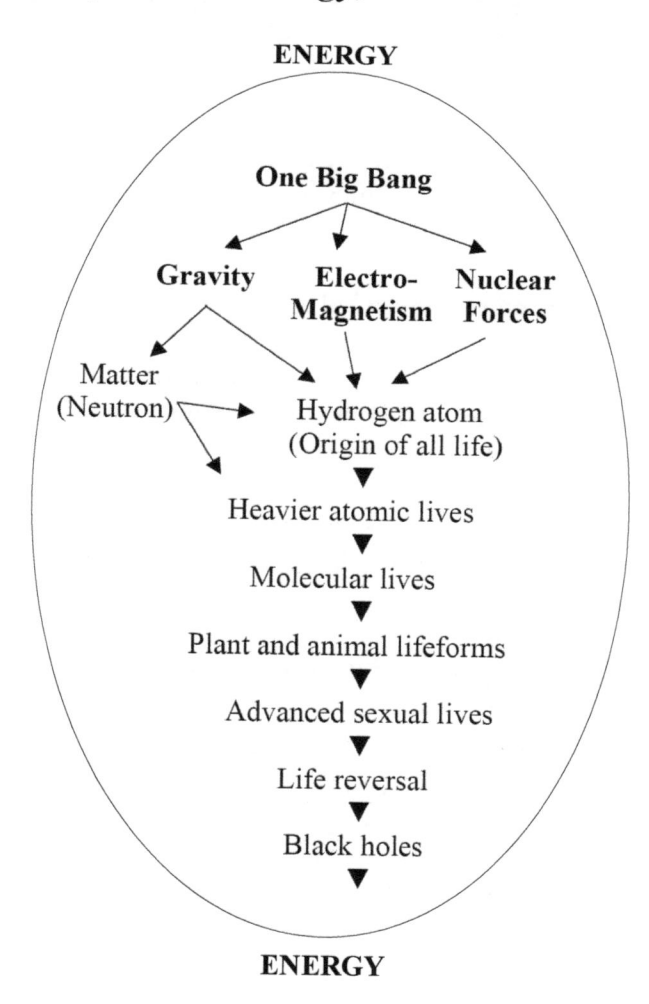

ENERGY

One Big Bang

Gravity   **Electro-Magnetism**   **Nuclear Forces**

Matter (Neutron) → Hydrogen atom (Origin of all life)
▼
Heavier atomic lives
▼
Molecular lives
▼
Plant and animal lifeforms
▼
Advanced sexual lives
▼
Life reversal
▼
Black holes
▼

ENERGY

8
MY TEN COMMANDMENTS

Strangely, during my final state of existence, my own understanding had expanded even beyond my universe. My ten commandments are for humans with open minds.

1. There is no religious God in our universe

It was the religious humans living on flat Earth who had created the different mysteries called God. No amount of their praying prevented any loss of religious lives from natural disasters on planet Earth. All religious beliefs are childish mentalities, but a few are the worst plagues on our planet. Some religious humans not only kill other humans that have other religious beliefs, but also kill humans in the same religion.

2. The starting point of life is the atom

It took humans a long period of existence before recognising that they lived on a planet and not a flat earth. After that, the humans also started recognising the stars, galaxies and the universe. Humans also advanced into creating the atom bomb. No human managed to recognise that the origin of life is the atom. That elementary fact is revealed in this book.

Energy is the Real God

3. Only human sex lives became unnatural

Humans are supposed to be the most advanced form of life on our planet. However, no human had recognised the cause that made us become the most degraded form of sex life on the planet. An explanation in the book of that unnatural behaviour will shock the most educated humans.

4. Money created by humans has degraded humanity

Only recent humans created the stupidity called money that is now totally plaguing both the human as well as numerous other natural lives on our planet. The supposedly most intelligent lifeforms are the only ones that are committing crimes. No natural form of life commits any crime and nor have they enslaved themselves to the stupidity called money.

5. Humanity has created global atmospheric disasters

The global atmosphere of our planet has been disturbed by us humans. The human discoveries of coal and oil reserves on the planet have been upsetting the speed of the normal processes of atmospheric changes. Coal and oil are only the remains of the plant lives that had been absorbing the energy from the sun for their survival and existence over millions of years. Human lives only are now using the ancient, trapped solar energy to speed up the climate change on our planet without being aware of the plagues we are creating on our unique planet.

6. Humans can experience death during life

The God concept was created only by humans who could not accept the termination of their existence. No human has recognised that death will be no different to what we all have been experiencing during their lives. Being in deep sleep or unconscious is no different to what you will be experiencing when you are dead. Death will be no different to not waking up after going to sleep. Goodnight folks.

7. Heaven and hell only during life

All humans who wish to be in a heaven after life should wake up to the fact that the experience of heaven is something they are missing out during their lives. Humans need to wake up from their state of dreaming during their lives in order to experience the real life on a unique planet. Humans who have any concept of an existence without a body also need to be aware that heaven also has a hell alongside, forever.

8. Non-sexual life will take over the advanced state of existence

The sexual lives on our planet were an advanced state of existence from the initial non-sexual lives that are still in existence. Due to the collapse of sexual life of the most advanced lifeforms on our planet, the evolution of life has started to create the advanced non-sexual life that is already in the process of emergence. Human sexual life problems will have been flushed out of existence by the emergence of the homo non-sexual.

9. Two galaxies may mate into another life.

In a few billion years, our Milky Way galaxy is likely to be uniting with the Andromeda galaxy. Later, they will be going into a black hole and back home from where they had come, the Creator of our universe called Energy.

10. Energy created matter and life.

Humans need to wake up to the fact that Energy is a far more logical and scientific understanding of our unique existence. It is what creates as well as participates with matter and life. Both matter and life rely entirely on some energy for their existence. Energy is simply our God that not only created us, but also has been with us and participates in all our life existences.

The God in any religious head is a Qwerty.
The God in both my body and my mind is Energy
Amen.

Addendum 1

FOREIGN WORDS

Aum ॐ is an Indian word that is made of three sounds. The '*A*' is produced by the throat, the '*u*' is like a 'oo' created in the roof of the mouth with the lifted tongue and the '*m*' is created by the closing lips. *Aum* is the holy sound that could be produced by the last breath of a human saying goodbye to life.

Amen 'So be it' in Hebrew

Addendum 2
THE BOOK COVER

The images and diagrams on the front cover of the book represent the creation of our universe from a black hole. The bolts of lightning represent the Big Bang explosion that created our universe which formed into stars in our galaxy. The important star is the sun that resulted in the creation of our lives.

The two faces are that of Albert Einstein and me that represent the pair whose thinking created the contents of this book.